To Lena
With Love
Wilson

The Treasure of Love

The Treasure
of Love

Hallmark Editions

Editorial Research: Shifra Stein
Editorial Direction: Aileene Neighbors

The publisher wishes to thank those who have given their kind permission to re-
print material included in this book. Every effort has been made to give proper
acknowledgments. Any omissions or errors are deeply regretted, and the pub-
lisher, upon notification, will be pleased to make necessary corrections in sub-
sequent editions.
Acknowledgments: 1 Corinthians 13 from the *King James Version Bible*. Re-
printed by permission of the Cambridge University Press. Published by the
Syndics of Cambridge University Press. "Afterwards" from *The Heart of Home* by
Anne Campbell. Reprinted by permission of the author. "Light alters day..." by
Paul Engle. © Paul Engle. Reprinted by permission of the author. Excerpts from
Autumn Love Song by Jesse Stuart. Copyright © 1971 by Hallmark Cards, Inc.
Excerpt from *Wind, Sand and Stars* by Antoine de Saint-Exupéry. Copyright 1939
by Antoine de Saint-Exupéry, renewed 1967 by Lewis Galantiere. Reprinted by
permission of the publishers, Harcourt Brace Jovanovich, Inc. "Explanations of
Love" by Carl Sandburg. From *Good Morning, America*, copyright, 1928, 1956, by
Carl Sandburg. Reprinted by permission of Harcourt Brace Jovanovich, Inc. Ex-
cerpt abridged from Letter from Mark Twain to Olivia Langdon, Buffalo, August
21, P.M. 1869 - in *The Love Letters of Mark Twain*, edited by Dixon Wecter. Copy-
right, 1947, 1949 by The Mark Twain Company. By permission of Harper & Row,
Publishers, Inc. "The Daisies" from *Collected Poems* by James Stephens. Copy-
right 1915 by Macmillan Publishing Co., Inc., renewed 1943 by James Stephens.
Reprinted with permission of Macmillan Publishing Co., Inc., Mrs. Iris Wise,
Macmillan London & Basingstoke, and The Macmillan Company of Canada
Limited. "Beauty" from *Poems* by John Masefield. Copyright 1912 by Macmillan
Publishing Co., Inc., renewed 1940 by John Masefield. Reprinted with permission
of Macmillan Publishing Co., Inc. and The Society of Authors as the literary
representative of the Estate of John Masefield. "The Beloved" is reprinted with
permission of Macmillan Publishing Co., Inc. from *Collected Poems* by Sara Teas-
dale. Copyright 1926 by Macmillan Publishing Co., Inc., renewed 1954 by Mamie
T. Wheless. "When" by Edwin Markham. Reprinted by permission of Mrs. Virgil
Markham. "By Messenger" and "Prime" from *The Complete Poetical Works of Amy
Lowell*. © 1955 by Houghton Mifflin Company, and reprinted with their permis-
sion. "My Love Comes Walking" by Mark Van Doren from *Collected and New
Poems*. © 1965 by Mark Van Doren. Published by Hill & Wang. Reprinted with
permission of Nannine Joseph, agent for the Estate of Mark Van Doren. Song of
Solomon 2:8-13 from the *Revised Standard Version Bible*. Reprinted by permis-
sion of the National Council of the Churches of Christ. "Love" by Roy Croft from
Best Loved Poems of the American People, selected by Hazel Felleman. © 1936,
Doubleday & Company, Inc. Reprinted with permission. "For Those Who Love"
from *The Poems of Henry van Dyke* by Henry van Dyke is reprinted by permis-
sion of Charles Scribner's Sons. Copyright 1911 Charles Scribner's Sons. "A
Lover's Envy" from *The White Bees* by Henry van Dyke is reprinted by permis-
sion of Charles Scribner's Sons. Copyright 1909 Charles Scribner's Sons.
© 1975, Hallmark Cards, Inc., Kansas City, Missouri.
Printed in the United States of America.
Library of Congress Catalog Card Number: 74-83760.
Standard Book Number: 87529-407-3.

AN INVITATION

Love is a world all its own — an experience almost beyond description, and yet so beautiful that writers throughout the ages have searched their hearts for ways to express its gentle moods and stirring emotions.

Passionately, tenderly they have written, each hoping to capture for all time the wonder of living in love's own special realm. You are invited now to share some of their most touching thoughts and poignant feelings in *The Treasure of Love.*

Here are William Shakespeare, Elizabeth Barrett Browning, Sara Teasdale, Emily Dickinson and others whose words of love have been gathered into a keepsake of rare delight. Come join them as they sing of sweet romance and whisper of lasting devotion. Let each page of this beautifully designed collection carry you further, deeper into that magic world true lovers know. Come listen with your heart!

This is the true measure of love,
    When we believe
That we alone can love,
    That no one could ever have
Loved so before us,
That no one will ever love
In the same way after us.

Johann Wolfgang von Goethe

Love is the tender branch on the tree of life.

William Webb

To be loved is to know
    happiness and contentment.
To give love is to know
    the joy of sharing oneself.
It is through the miracle of love
    that we discover
    the fullness of life.

Barbara Burrow

5

BEAUTY

I have seen dawn and sunset
   on moors and windy hills
Coming in solemn beauty
   like slow old tunes of Spain;
I have seen the lady April
   bringing daffodils,
Bringing the springing grass
   and the soft warm April rain.

I have heard the song of the blossoms
   and the old chant of the sea,
And seen strange lands
   from under the arched white sails of ships;
But the loveliest things of beauty
   God ever has shown to me,
Are her voice, and her hair, and eyes,
   and the dear red curve of her lips.

John Masefield

Life is a peaceful walk through quiet meadows,
   a song of joy, a sun-kissed morning,
   a star-swept sky, a new world dawning...
   when you're in love.

Barbara Plumb

IF THOU MUST LOVE ME

If thou must love me, let it be for nought
Except for love's sake only. Do not say
"I love her for her smile — her look — her way
Of speaking gently, for a trick of thought
That falls in well with mine, and certes brought
A sense of pleasant ease on such a day" —
For these things in themselves, Beloved, may
Be changed, or change for thee, and love, so wrought,
May be unwrought so. Neither love me for
Thine own dear pity's wiping my cheeks dry,
A creature might forget to weep, who bore
Thy comfort long, and lose thy love thereby!
But love me for love's sake, that evermore
Thou mayest love on, through love's eternity.

Elizabeth Barrett Browning

Love is never lost.
If not reciprocated, it will flow back and soften
and purify the heart.

Washington Irving

THE SILENT VOICE

Love hath a language of his own —
   A voice that goes
From heart to heart — whose mystic tone
   Love only knows.

The lotus flower, whose leaves I now
   Kiss silently,
Far more than words will tell thee how
   I worship thee.

The mirror, which to thee I hold —
   Which, when impressed
With thy bright looks, I turn and fold
   To this fond breast —

Doth it not speak, beyond all spells
   Of poet's art,
How deep thy hidden image dwells
   In this hushed heart?

Thomas Moore

Love is the heart in blossom.

Myrtle Reed

TO MY VALENTINE

I wish you always
in your heart
like the chime
of silver bells
the rapture and
the rhapsody
of love, whose music
gives meaning
to the rhythm of life.

Kay Wissinger

NEAR

Yours is a little love
Compared to that great force
In which all lesser loves
Have all their root and source.

But your love is near
And whispers to my heart
Of that infinite love,
Of which it is a part.

Clara Aiken Speer

HOW DO I LOVE THEE?

How do I love thee? Let me count the ways.
I love thee to the depth and breadth and height
My soul can reach, when feeling out of sight
For the ends of Being and ideal Grace.
I love thee to the level of every day's
Most quiet need, by sun and candlelight.
I love thee freely, as men strive for Right;
I love thee purely, as they turn from Praise.
I love thee with the passion put to use
In my old griefs, and with my childhood's faith.
I love thee with a love I seemed to lose
With my lost saints — I love thee with the breath,
Smiles, tears, of all my life! — and, if God choose,
I shall but love thee better after death.

Elizabeth Barrett Browning

...For I do love you...
as the dew loves the flowers;
as the birds love the sunshine;
as the wavelets love the breeze....
Mark Twain

SUN-WORSHIP

If I were the rose at your window,
Happiest rose of its crew,
Every blossom I bore would bend inward,
They'd know where the sunshine grew.

James Russell Lowell

Up, up again,
    Until the ridge plateau is won,
    Our highest level under the sun;
    And any way we look, on every side,
    We see so high and far,
    The moon, the sun and star

Will seem close by our side.

We know that love
    is high and deep and wide.

Up now, where love gone out of bounds
Will let us see
How high, how wide,
    how deep is this eternity.

Jesse Stuart

THE GARDEN

What makes a garden?
Flowers, grass and trees,
Fragrance, grace and color:
Lovely gifts like these.

What makes a garden
And why do gardens grow?
Love lives in gardens —
God and lovers know!

Caroline Giltinan

THE MAGIC OF LOVE

Love…
     sings its own music,
     writes its own rhyme,
     paints its own rainbow,
     counts its own time.
Love…
     smiles its own gladness,
     laughs its own fun,
     dreams its own heaven,
     shines its own sun.

Karen Ravn

A RED, RED ROSE

O, my luve's like a red, red rose
    That's newly sprung in June;
O, my luve's like the melodie
    That's sweetly played in tune.

As fair thou art, my bonnie lass,
    So deep in luve am I;
And I will luve thee still, my dear,
    Till a' the seas gang dry.

Till a' the seas gang dry, my dear,
    And the rocks melt wi' the sun;
I will luve thee still, my dear,
    While the sands o' life shall run.

Robert Burns

At the very touch of love
    everyone becomes a poet.

Plato

TO LOVE YOU

To love you
  is to love the trees,
  is to love the warm
  and gentle breeze,
  is to love the world I see…
To love you
  is to love the days,
  is to love the morning's
  warming rays
  and the night's tranquility…
To love you
  is to love to live,
  is to love to share,
  and care and give
  and it's wanting to be me…
To love you.

Mary Walley

There are explanations of love in all languages
  and not one found wiser than this:
  There is a place where love begins and a place
  where love ends — and love asks nothing.

Carl Sandburg

SHALL I COMPARE THEE TO A SUMMER'S DAY?

Shall I compare thee to a summer's day?
Thou art more lovely and more temperate.
Rough winds do shake the darling buds of May,
And summer's lease hath all too short a date:
Sometime too hot the eye of heaven shines,
And often is his gold complexion dimm'd;
And every fair from fair sometime declines,
By chance, or nature's changing course, untrimm'd;
But thy eternal summer shall not fade
Nor lose possession of that fair thou owest;
Nor shall Death brag thou wander'st in his shade,
When in eternal lines to time thou grow'st.
    So long as men can breathe or eyes can see,
    So long lives this, and this gives life to thee.

William Shakespeare

The fountain of love
   is the rose and the lily, the sun and the dove.

Heinrich Heine

SHE WALKS IN BEAUTY

She walks in beauty, like the night
Of cloudless climes and starry skies;
And all that's best of dark and bright
Meet in her aspect and her eyes:
Thus mellowed to that tender light
Which heaven to gaudy day denies.

One shade the more, one ray the less,
Had half impaired the nameless grace
Which waves in every raven tress,
Or softly lightens o'er her face;
Where thoughts serenely sweet express
How pure, how dear, their dwelling place.

And on that cheek, and o'er that brow,
So soft, so calm, yet eloquent,
The smiles that win, the tints that glow,
But tell of days in goodness spent,
A mind at peace with all below,
A heart whose love is innocent!

George Gordon, Lord Byron

SPRING SONNET

I've never known a spring like this before,
Though I have seen so many come and go.
The violets show in lovely purple clusters
And every cherry branch like drifts of snow.
The yellow jonquils nod to passing strangers,
While lilacs fill the air with sweet perfume;
The tulip bulbs that slept have now awakened
And line the walk with dazzling crimson bloom.

Other springs I had not viewed your loveliness,
Or thought that you were more than passing fair;
But now, with bridal wreath in bloom beside you
And stray, white petals nestling in your hair,
Like songbirds on the wing, my spirits soar;
I've never known a spring like this before.

Reginald Holmes

Love is a symbol of eternity.
It wipes out all sense of time,
destroying all memory of a beginning
and all fear of an end.

Anne Louise de Stael

I GAVE MYSELF

I gave myself to him,
And took himself for pay.
The solemn contract of life
Was ratified this way.

The wealth might disappoint,
Myself a poorer prove
Than this great purchaser suspect,
The daily own of Love.

Depreciate the vision;
But, till the merchant buy,
Still fable, in the isles of spice,
The subtle cargoes lie.

At least, 'tis mutual risk, —
Some found it mutual gain;
Sweet debt of Life, — each night to owe,
Insolvent, every noon.

Emily Dickinson

Of all the music that reaches farthest into heaven,
it is the beating of a loving heart.

Henry Ward Beecher

LOVE'S PHILOSOPHY

The fountains mingle with the river
   And the rivers with the ocean,
The winds of heaven mix forever
With a sweet emotion;
Nothing in the world is single,
All things by a law divine
In one another's being mingle —
Why not I with thine?

See the mountains kiss high heaven,
And the waves clasp one another;
No sister-flower would be forgiven
If it disdain'd its brother;
And the sunlight clasps the earth,
And the moonbeams kiss the sea —
What are all these kissings worth,
If thou kiss not me?

Percy Bysshe Shelley

What's the earth
With all its art, verse, music, worth —
Compared with love, found, gained and kept?

Robert Browning

21

WHAT IS LOVE?

To love very much is to love inadequately; we love — that
is all. Love cannot be modified without being nullified. Love
is a short word but it contains everything. Love means the
body, the soul, the life, the entire being. We feel love as we
feel the warmth of our blood, we breathe love as we breathe
the air, we hold it in ourselves as we hold our thoughts.
Nothing more exists for us. Love is not a word; it is a word-
less state indicated by four letters.

Guy de Maupassant

SILENCE

The briefest glance...
    the slightest touch
    to those in love
    can say so much...
The highest heights
    two hearts
    can reach
    come wordless...
    come through silent speech.

Barbara Burrow

I have your picture in my room; I never pass it without
stopping to look at it; and yet when you are present with me
I scarce ever cast my eyes on it. If a picture, which is but
a mute representation of an object, can give such pleasure,
what cannot letters inspire? They have souls; they can
speak; they have in them all that force which expresses
the transports of the heart; they have all the fire of our
passions, they can raise them as much as if the persons
themselves were present; they have all the tenderness and
the delicacy of speech, and sometimes even a boldness of
expression beyond it.

Letter from Heloise to Abelard

LIGHTED LAMP

Love is something eternal —
              the aspect may change, but not the essence.
        There is the same difference in a person
              before and after he is in love
as there is in an unlighted lamp and one that is burning.
        The lamp was there and it was a good lamp,
                 but now it is shedding light, too,
                     and that is its real function.

Vincent van Gogh

And I shall dream both before and after I go to sleep, of the little flower that has sprung up in the desert beside me and shed its fragrance over my life and made its ways attractive with its beauty and turned its weariness to contentment with its sweet spirit. And I shall bless you, my darling, out of a fullness of a heart that knows your worth beyond the ken of any…better than all others I can love you, and do love you, and shall always love you, always. Good night, darling—and peaceful slumbers refresh you and ministering angels attend you.

Letter from Mark Twain to his wife, Olivia Langdon

FOR THOSE WHO LOVE

Time is…
  Too slow for those who wait,
 Too swift for those who fear,
  Too long for those who grieve,
   Too short for those who rejoice;
 But for those who love,
  Time is not.

Henry van Dyke

FIRST FLAME

Ah, I remember well — and how can I
    But ever more remember well — when first
    Our flame began, when scarce we knew what was
    The flame we felt; when as we sat and sighed,
    And looked upon each other, and conceived
    Not what we ailed, yet something we did ail,
    And yet were well, and yet we were not well,
    And what was our disease we could not tell.
    Then would we kiss, then sigh, then look: and thus
    In that first garden of our simpleness
    We spent our childhood: but when years began
    To reap the fruit of knowledge, ah, how then
    Would she with graver looks, with sweet stern brow,
    Check my presumption and my forwardness;
    Yet still would give me flowers, still would shew
    What she would have me, yet not have me, know.

Samuel Daniel

Love does not consist in gazing at each other
    but in looking outward together
        in the same direction.

Antoine de Saint-Exupéry

I WISH I COULD REMEMBER THAT FIRST DAY

I wish I could remember that first day,
First hour, first moment of your meeting me,
If bright or dim the season, it might be
Summer or winter for aught I can say;
So unrecorded did it slip away,
So blind was I to see and to foresee,
So dull to mark the budding of my tree
That would not blossom yet for many a May.
If only I could recollect it, such
A day of days! I let it come and go
As traceless as a thaw of bygone snow;
It seemed to mean so little, meant so much;
If only now I could recall that touch,
First touch of hand in hand — did one but know!

Christina Rossetti

True love's the gift which God has given
   To man alone beneath the heaven:
   The silver link, the silken tie,
   Which heart to heart and mind to mind
   In body and in soul can bind.

Sir Walter Scott

COLOR IT LOVE

Golden was the day at dawning,
Brilliant was the morning sky,
Azure were the hours of promise,
Crimson tipped, the clouds on high.
Streaked with shadow was the evening,
Dusky was the gentle night,
Iridescent was each moment,
Touched with joy and love and light.

Doris Chalma Brock

Your lips, so like the color
    of the russet dogwood leaf,
In our love's journey
    we must not forget to kiss,
The season of the summer's blossoming
    is brief,
The season is uncertain for the petal
    and the leaf.

We must, we must, take time,
    take time, to kiss;
If we do not,
We miss.

Love is a hundred lives.

Jesse Stuart

A LOVER'S ENVY

I envy every flower that blows
  Beside the pathway where she goes,
  And every bird that sings to her,
  And every breeze that brings to her
  The fragrance of the rose.

I envy every poet's rhyme
That moves her heart at eventime,
  And every tree that wears for her
  Its brightest bloom, and bears for her
  The fruitage of its prime.

I envy every Southern night
That paves her path with moonbeams white,
  And silvers all the leaves for her,
  And in their shadow weaves for her
  A dream of dear delight.

I envy none whose love requires
Of her a gift, a task that tires:
  I only long to live to her,
  I only ask to give to her
  All that her heart desires.

Henry van Dyke

HARMONY

Sometimes it seems
    our two hearts beat as one
In perfect time.
Your breath and mine
    are drawn in unison,
And our sighs rhyme.
Because of this, all
The world's in harmony:
The songs of birds
Are learned from our singing,
    and all poetry
Echoes our words.

Barbara Kunz Loots

EROS

The sense of the world is short,
Long and various the report,
    To love and be beloved;
Men and gods have not outlearned it;
And, how oft soe'er they've turned it,
    'Tis not to be improved.

Ralph Waldo Emerson

LOVE FOR ALL SEASONS

As soft and gentle
    as a summer breeze...
    as radiant and beautiful
    as Autumn
    in all its finery...
    as warm and friendly
    as a cozy fire
    on a frosty winter night...
    as refreshing and delightful
    as the springtime flowers...
    you are my love for all seasons!
                Barbara Plumb

Whatever woman may cast her lot with mine,
            should any ever do so,
    it is my intention to do all in my power
            to make her happy and contented;
and there is nothing I can imagine
        that would make me more unhappy
                than to fail in the effort.
                Abraham Lincoln

31

THE INDIAN SERENADE

I arise from dreams of thee
  In the first sweet sleep of night,
  When the winds are breathing low,
  And the stars are shining bright;
  I arise from dreams of thee,
  And a spirit in my feet
  Hath led me — who knows how?
  To thy chamber window, Sweet!

  The wandering airs they faint
  On the dark, the silent stream —
  The Champak odors fail
  Like sweet thoughts in a dream;
  The nightingale's complaint,
  It dies upon her heart —
  As I must on thine,
  Oh, beloved as thou art!

  Oh lift me from the grass!
  I die! I faint! I fail!
  Let thy love in kisses rain
  On my lips and eyelids pale.
  My cheek is cold and white, alas!
  My heart beats loud and fast —
  Oh! press it to thine own again,
  Where it will break at last.

Percy Bysshe Shelley

THE VOICE OF MY BELOVED

The voice of my beloved!
　　Behold, he comes,
　　　　leaping upon the mountains,
　　　　bounding over the hills.
My beloved is like a gazelle,
　　or a young stag.
Behold, there he stands
　　behind our wall,
　　　　gazing in at the windows,
　　　　looking through the lattice.
My beloved speaks and says to me:
　　"Arise, my love, my fair one,
　　and come away;
　　　　for lo, the winter is past,
　　　　the rain is over and gone.
The flowers appear on the earth,
　　the time of singing has come,
　　　　and the voice of the turtledove
　　　　is heard in our land.
The fig tree puts forth its figs,
　　and the vines are in blossom;
　　　　they give forth fragrance.
Arise, my love, my fair one,
　　and come away."

Song of Solomon 2:8-13

THE WORLD IS FULL OF BEAUTY

There is beauty in the sunlight,
   And the soft blue heaven above;
      Oh, the world is full of beauty
         When the heart is full of love.
           W. L. Smith

WHEN

When I wait for your face
   In some garden apart,
Little songs of your grace
   Carol into my heart.

When I hear the loved sound
   Of your feet that delay,
I am lifted and crowned
   On the peaks of the day.
       Edwin Markham

Love conquers all.
Virgil

LOVE

I love you,
　　Not only for what you are,
　　But for what I am
　　When I am with you.

I love you,
Not only for what
You have made of yourself,
But for what
You are making of me.

I love you
For the part of me
That you bring out;
I love you
For putting your hand
Into my heaped-up heart
And passing over
All the foolish, weak things
That you can't help
Dimly seeing there,
And for drawing out
Into the light
All the beautiful belongings
That no one else had looked
Quite far enough to find....

I love you
Because you have done
More than any creed
Could have done
To make me good,
And more than any fate
Could have done
To make me happy.

Roy Croft

THE HEART

The heart hath its own memory,
    like the mind,
And in it are enshrined
The precious keepsakes,
    into which is wrought
The giver's loving thought.

Henry Wadsworth Longfellow

THE GARDEN OF LOVE

I went to the Garden of Love
And saw what I never had seen:
A Chapel was built in the midst,
Where I used to play on the green.

And the gates of this Chapel were shut,
And "Thou shalt not" writ over the door;
So I turned to the Garden of Love
That so many sweet flowers bore;

And I saw it was filled with graves,
And tombstones where flowers should be;
And priests in black gowns were walking their rounds,
And binding with briars my joys and desires.
William Blake

Love is a circle, that doth restless move
  In the same sweet eternity of love.
Robert Herrick

TO CELIA

Drink to me only with thine eyes,
    And I will pledge with mine;
Or leave a kiss but in the cup,
    And I'll not look for wine.
The thirst that from the soul doth rise
    Doth ask a drink divine;
But might I of Jove's nectar sup,
    I would not change for thine.

I sent thee late a rosy wreath,
    Not so much honoring thee
As giving it a hope that there
    It could not withered be.
But thou thereon didst only breathe,
    And sent'st it back to me;
Since when it grows, and smells, I swear,
    Not of itself but thee.

Ben Jonson

Grace was in all her steps, heaven in her eye,
In every gesture dignity and love.

John Milton

SUMMUM BONUM

All the breath and the bloom of the year
    in the bag of one bee:
All the wonder and wealth of the mine
    in the heart of one gem:
In the core of one pearl all the shade
    and the shine of the sea;
Breath and bloom, shade and shine,
    wonder, wealth, and — how far above them —
      Truth, that's brighter than gem,
      Trust, that's purer than pearl,
Brightest truth, purest trust in the universe —
    all were for me in the kiss of one girl.

Robert Browning

It's all I have to bring today,
This, and my heart beside,
This, and my heart, and all the fields,
And all the meadows wide.
Be sure you count, should I forget, —
Some one the sum could tell, —
This, and my heart, and all the bees
Which in the clover dwell.

Emily Dickinson

SECRET LOVE

I feed a flame within, which so torments me
That it both pains my heart, and yet contents me:
'Tis such a pleasing smart, and I so love it,
That I had rather die than once remove it.

Yet he for whom I grieve shall never know it;
My tongue does not betray, nor my eyes show it,
Not a sigh, nor a tear, my pain discloses,
But they fall silently, like dew on roses.

Thus, to prevent my Love from being cruel,
My heart's the sacrifice, as 'tis the fuel;
And while I suffer this to give him quiet,
My faith rewards my love, though he deny it.

On his eyes will I gaze, and there delight me;
While I conceal my love no frown can fright me.
To be more happy I dare not aspire,
Nor can I fall more low, mounting no higher.

John Dryden

Look down and bless them from above
    And keep their hearts alight with love.

Robert Hugh Benson

41

AFTERWARDS

Afterwards it is not the kiss we remember —
Only that one day in gold September
Your spirit met my spirit, and we clung
Together — wordless for one moment, hung
In space....Afterwards recalling — not the greeting,
And not the kiss...but just our spirits meeting!
Anne Campbell

Who can doubt that we exist only to love?
    Disguise it,
       in fact, as we will, we love without intermission.
Where we seem most effectually to shut out love,
       it lies covert and concealed:
     we live not a moment exempt from its influence.
Blaise Pascal

Light alters day. Love alters us. We are
The woman and the man each knew before,
But changed by love's abruptness, as a dark
Room burns with sunlight from an opened door.
Paul Engle

42

IN THE SPRING

In the Spring a fuller crimson
    comes upon the robin's breast;
In the Spring the wanton lapwing
    gets himself another crest;
In the Spring a livelier iris
    changes on the burnish'd dove;
In the Spring a young man's fancy
    lightly turns to thoughts of love.
                        Alfred, Lord Tennyson

All that a man has to say or do
        that can possibly concern mankind,
is in some shape or other to tell the story of his love —
    to sing, and, if he is fortunate and keeps alive,
                he will be forever in love.
                        Henry David Thoreau

Happiness is only in loving.
                Leo Tolstoy

THE DAISIES

In the scented bud of the morning — O,
    When the windy grass went rippling far!
I saw my dear one walking slow
    In the field where the daisies are.

We did not laugh, and we did not speak,
    As we wandered happily, to and fro;
I kissed my dear on either cheek,
    In the bud of the morning — O.

A lark sang up, from the breezy land;
    A lark sang down, from a cloud afar;
And she and I went, hand in hand,
    In the field where the daisies are.

James Stephens

There is nothing holier in this life of ours
    than the first consciousness of love —
the first fluttering of its silken wings —
    the first rising sound and breath of that wind
which is so soon to sweep through the soul.

Henry Wadsworth Longfellow

PRIME

Your voice is like bells over roofs at dawn
    When a bird flies
    And the sky changes to a fresher colour.

Speak, speak, Beloved.
Say little things
For my ears to catch
And run with them to my heart.
                                                    Amy Lowell

BEQUEST

I give you the scent of the woodbine,
The curve of a gull in flight,
The first pale star of the evening
For your heart's innermost delight.

I give you the song of the redbird,
The pale, slim moon up above,
And the twilight hush for dreaming;
I give you my love, my love.
                                                    Kay Wissinger

IF I COULD CAPTURE A POEM FOR YOU

If I Could Capture a Poem For You —

Like a photograph captures a scene —
I would put into it sea green thoughts
        about to break
    On a windswept, bleached sand beach.
I would have cloud words —
                majestically building
                    into great banks
Against a blue, blue sky.
And in the foreground —
            sun drenched with light —
I would frame a closeup thought
                of you
Like a white-winged bird
            in
                flight.
                    Patricia White

I love you for the sake of what you are,
    And not of what you do.
            Jean Ingelow

TOO YOUNG FOR LOVE

Too young for love?
Ah, say not so!
Tell reddening rosebuds not to blow!
Wait not for spring to pass away,
Love's summer months begin with May!
Too young for love?
Ah, say not so!
Too young? Too young?
Ah, no! No! No!

Too young for love?
Ah, say not so,
While daisies bloom and tulips glow!
June soon will come with lengthened day
To practice all love learned in May.
Too young for love?
Ah, say not so!
Too young? Too young?
Ah, no! No! No!

Oliver Wendell Holmes

You must get your living by loving.
Henry David Thoreau

48

THE LEGEND OF THE ROSE

Many years ago, there lived a beautiful princess named Rosamond. Dozens of princely suitors sought her hand in marriage, bringing her rich and wonderful gifts as a sign of their love. But none of the suitors or their gifts seemed to please Rosamond. One day, a prince from a faraway country came to the palace. He had heard of Rosamond's beauty and her gentle ways, and he hoped she might consent to be his wife.

The gift he brought was neither gold nor precious jewels. It was a single flower, one the princess had never seen before. The prince called it a "rose." Rosamond was delighted with the flower's rare beauty and fragrance.

The prince had chosen the rose for Rosamond because it was the only way he knew to tell one so beautiful of his love. Touched by the prince's gift, by the depth of his affection, Rosamond pledged her love to him for all of her life.

Thus, according to this legend, the rose became the flower of love, and it has symbolized abiding love between men and women ever since the time of Rosamond.

Love, to endure life's sorrow and earth's woe,
   Needs friendship's solid masonry below.
                                    Ella Wheeler Wilcox

LOVE

Love is a private country of the heart,
  Where none but lovers can come in or stay;
  You cannot find it marked on any chart
  Or hire a guide to take you there for pay.
  But lovers navigate by dreams, love wise
  And find their path by stars that are their own.
  Somewhere past all known worlds love's country lies!
  Worlds may crowd close, but lovers are alone
  And speak in silences no grosser ear
  Alien to love can ever understand.
  Love is its own celestial hemisphere,
  And lovers, citizens of no known land.
  Look in a crowded room how lovers are
  As if they stood upon another star.

James Dillet Freeman

  Love knows no time nor place
  Love is...
  Open and free
  Growing, changing
  Soaring to new heights
  Love knows no bounds, no limits
  Love is.

Katherine Hollingshead

50

LOVE SONG

Come walk with me
  As twilight falls,
  And crimson splashes in the sky;
  In shadowed pathways,
  You and I
  Can walk and dream.

  And high upon some windblown cliff
  Which overlooks the sea,
  Come watch with me
  The restive waves,
  That spill upon the sand...
  Come closer, Love,
  Give me your hand.

  And as the sun's last rays
  Take flight,
  And evening melts into the night,
  Keep vigil here
  Beneath the stars
  Which shimmer on the shore...
  Then kiss me, Dear,
  Once more, once more...

Locked in your arms,
My being sings,
And every dream that I have known
Comes true, for
I am yours alone.

Katherine Nelson Davis

THE BELOVED

It is enough of honor for one lifetime
   To have known you better than the rest have known,
The shadows and the colors of your voice,
   Your will, immutable and still as stone.

The shy heart, so lonely and so gay,
   The sad laughter and the pride of pride,
The tenderness, the depth of tenderness
   Rich as the earth, and wide as heaven is wide.

Sara Teasdale

LOVE LETTER

My dearest Girl, This moment I have set myself to copy some
verses out fair. I cannot proceed with any degree of content.
I must write you a line or two and see if that will assist in
dismissing you from my Mind for ever so short a time. Upon
my Soul I can think of nothing else. The time is passed when
I had power to advise and warn you against the unpromising
morning of my Life. My love has made me selfish. I cannot
exist without you. I am forgetful of every thing but seeing
you again — my Life seems to stop there — I see no further.
You have absorb'd me. I have a sensation at the present
moment as though I was dissolving — I should be exquisitely
miserable without the hope of soon seeing you. I should be
afraid to separate myself far from you. My sweet Fanny,
will your heart never change? My love, will it? I have no
limit now to my love — Your note came in just here — I
cannot be happier away from you. 'Tis richer than an
Argosy of Pearles. Do not threat me even in jest. I have been
astonished that Men could die Martyrs for religion — I
have shudder'd at it. I shudder no more — I could be
martyr'd for my Religion — Love is my religion — I could
die for that. I could die for you. My Creed is Love and you
are its only tenet. You have ravish'd me away by a Power
I cannot resist; and yet I could resist till I saw you; and ever
since I have seen you I have endeavoured often 'to reason
against the reasons of my Love'. I can do that no
more — the pain would be too great. My love is selfish.
I cannot breathe without you. Yours for ever,

John Keats, Letter to Fanny Brawne, 1819

Love much. Earth has enough of bitter in it.
  Cast sweets into its cup whene'er you can.
No heart so hard but love at last may win it...
  Love on, through doubt and darkness; and believe
  There is no thing which love may not achieve.
Ella Wheeler Wilcox

BY MESSENGER

One night
  When there was a clear moon,
  I sat down
  To write a poem
  About maple trees.
  But the dazzle of moonlight
  In the ink
  Blinded me,
  And I could only write
  What I remembered.
  Therefore, on the wrapping of my poem
  I have inscribed your name.
Amy Lowell

MY LOVE COMES WALKING

My love comes walking,
And these flowers
That never saw her til this day
Look up; but then
Bend down straightway.

My love sees nothing
Here but me,
Who never trembled thus before;
And glances down
Lest I do more.

My love is laughing;
Those wild things
Were never tame until I too,
Down-dropping, kissed
Her silvery shoe.

Mark Van Doren

When we say yes to love…
We say hello to life.

Michael Anderson

56

I don't love you, not at all; on the contrary, I detest you —
You're a naughty, gawky, foolish Cinderella. You never
write me; you don't love your husband, you know what
pleasure your letters give him, and yet you haven't written
him six lines, dashed off casually!

What do you do all day, Madam? What is the affair so
important as to leave you no time to write to your devoted
lover? What affection stifles and puts to one side the love,
the tender and constant love you promised him? Of what
sort can be that marvelous being, that new lover who absorbs
every moment, tyrannizes over your days, and prevents your
giving any attention to your husband? Josephine, take care!
Some fine night, the doors will be broken open, and there
I'll be.

Indeed, I am very uneasy, my love, at receiving no
news of you; write me quickly four pages, pages full of
agreeable things which shall fill my heart with the
pleasantest feelings.

I hope before long to crush you in my arms and cover you
with a million kisses burning as though beneath the equator.

Love letter from Napoleon to Josephine

TRUE LOVE
from LOVE

True Love is but a humble, lowborn thing,
    And hath its food served up in earthenware;
    It is a thing to walk with, hand in hand,
    Through the everydayness of this work-day world,
    Baring its tender feet to every flint,
    Yet letting not one heartbeat go astray
    From Beauty's law of plainness and content;
    A simple, fireside thing, whose quiet smile
    Can warm earth's poorest hovel to a home....
    Such is true Love, which steals into the heart
    With feet as silent as the lightsome dawn
    That kisses smooth the rough brows of the dark,
    And hath its will through blissful gentleness,
    Not like a rocket, which, with passionate glare,
    Whirs suddenly up, then bursts, and leaves the night
    Painfully quivering on the dazed eyes;
    A love that gives and takes, that seeth faults,
    Not with flaw-seeking eyes like needle points,
    But loving-kindly ever looks them down
    With the o'ercoming faith that still forgives;
    A love that shall be new and fresh each hour,
    As is the sunset's golden mystery
    Or the sweet coming of the evening star,
    Alike, and yet most unlike, every day,
    And seeming ever best and fairest now....

James Russell Lowell

Enter Juliet above at a window.

Romeo: But, soft! What light through yonder window breaks?
It is the east, and Juliet is the sun.
Arise, fair sun, and kill the envious moon,
Who is already sick and pale with grief
That thou her maid art far more fair than she.
Be not her maid, since she is envious;
Her vestal livery is but sick and green,
And none but fools do wear it; cast it off.
It is my lady; O, it is my love!
O that she knew she were!
She speaks, yet she says nothing. What of that?
Her eye discourses; I will answer it.
I am too bold, 'tis not to me she speaks;
Two of the fairest stars in all the heaven,
Having some business, do entreat her eyes
To twinkle in their spheres till they return.
What if her eyes were there, they in her head?
The brightness of her cheek would shame those stars,
As daylight doth a lamp; her eyes in heaven
Would through the airy region stream so bright
That birds would sing, and think it were not night.
See how she leans her cheek upon her hand!
O that I were a glove upon that hand,
That I might touch that cheek!
Juliet: Ay me!
Romeo: She speaks.

O, speak again, bright angel, for thou art
as glorious to this night, being o'er my head,
As is a winged messenger of heaven
Unto the white-upturned wond'ring eyes
Of mortals that fall back to gaze on him,
When he bestrides the lazy-pacing clouds
And sails upon the bosom of the air.
Juliet: O Romeo, Romeo! wherefore art thou Romeo?
Deny thy father and refuse thy name;
Or, if thou wilt not, be but sworn my love,
And I'll no longer be a Capulet.
Romeo: (*Aside.*) Shall I hear more, or shall I
speak at this?
Juliet: 'Tis but thy name that is my enemy;
Thou art thyself, though not a Montague.
What's Montague? It is nor hand, nor foot,
Nor arm, nor face, nor any other part
Belonging to a man. O, be some other name!
What's in a name? That which we call a rose
By any other name would smell as sweet;
So Romeo would, were he not Romeo call'd
Retain that dear perfection which he owes
Without that title. Romeo, doff thy name;
And for thy name, which is no part of thee,
Take all myself.

from Romeo and Juliet *by William Shakespeare*

61

Set in Bodoni Book, a typeface designed by Giambattista Bodoni.
The paper is Hallmark Eggshell.
Designed by Myron McVay.